Greetings from New Orleans
A History in Postcards

Vaults of Old St. Louis Cemetery
New Orleans, La.

Carondelet Street, New Orleans, La.

Maskers on Float of Rex Parade, Mardi Gras Day, New Orleans, La.

Tina Skinner & Mary L. Martin

Schiffer Publishing Ltd ®

4880 Lower Valley Road, Atglen, PA 19310 USA

Published by Schiffer Publishing Ltd.
4880 Lower Valley Road
Atglen, PA 19310
Phone: (610) 593-1777; Fax: (610) 593-2002
E-mail: Info@schifferbooks.com

For the largest selection of fine reference books on this and related subjects,
please visit our web site at **www.schifferbooks.com**
We are always looking for people to write books on new and related subjects. If
you have an idea for a book please contact us at the above address.

This book may be purchased from the publisher.
Include $3.95 for shipping.
Please try your bookstore first.
You may write for a free catalog.

In Europe, Schiffer books are distributed by
Bushwood Books
6 Marksbury Ave.
Kew Gardens
Surrey TW9 4JF England
Phone: 44 (0) 20 8392-8585; Fax: 44 (0) 20 8392-9876
E-mail: info@bushwoodbooks.co.uk
Free postage in the U.K., Europe; air mail at cost.

Designed by Mark David Bowyer
Type set in Prose Antique / Dutch801 Rm BT

ISBN: 0-7643-2371-7
Printed in China

Contents

Temple Sinai, New Orleans, La.

Historical Overview

New Orleans has been, by turns, French, Spanish, and, very nearly, British. As one of the main ports of entry for the Southern United States, it has experienced waves of immigration, as well as ethnic tensions, and, worst of all, a devastating Union invasion. Imported prostitutes and exported sugar and cotton have taken turns in bolstering its economy. Mardi Gras, home-grown jazz, and a lush garden culture have sealed its reputation as one of the most colorful cities on the planet.

Though it would eventually become the largest city in the south, New Orleans got a slow start. French settlers were in the area for 36 years before the first residents called the site of the city their home. In 1721, Adrien de Pauger, a French engineer, laid out a plan for the French Quarter behind levees built to hold back the Mississippi. Two years later, the capital of the colony was relocated in New Orleans from Biloxi.

Germans and Swiss were lured to the city by campaigns touting the city as a paradise, which it wasn't, and in lieu of enough immigration, the French Government deported criminals and prostitutes to help populate the town.

Within forty years, river traffic was vastly expanded, and New Orleans was doing a brisk trade in indigo, sugar, rum, skins, and fur exports.

The French gave up their ambitions in North America in 1763, with the end of the Seven Year War, and Alexander O'Reilly, an Irish-born Spanish general arrived to forcibly take control of the city in 1769. When fire swept through the French Quarter in 1788, destroying more than 850 buildings, the government decreed that all buildings of two or more stories must be constructed of brick. The newly built city thus took on a much more Mediterranean appearance. The population, too, took on a new character as plantation owners and slaves arrived, fleeing the slave uprising in Saint Domingue (now Haiti) in 1791. With them came both the plantation economy, West Indian-style architecture, and voodoo.

Though Spain ceded Louisiana to France in 1800, Napoleon quickly sold it to the United States in order to finance his wars. Louisiana was officially admitted into the Union in 1812, just six weeks before the United States declared war on Great Britain. New Orleans fell under attack by British forces in 1815. General Andrew Jackson beat back the British, with a band of pirates, frontiersmen, French gentlemen, and free blacks.

Waves of newcomers began arriving that year, along with the first steamboat to ply the waters of New Orleans in 1812. Commercial growth in cotton and sugar, indigo, coffee, and bananas drove the population, but friction between the French Creoles and the Americans gave rise to the creation of an American section uptown, separated from the French Quarter by the neutral territory of Canal Street.

By the mid-1830s, the city had become the cotton capital of the world, and the second largest income-generating port in the nation after New York. By the 1860s, it was the largest city in the South. New Orleans annexed the city of Lafayette (now the garden district) and was cultivating a reputation for easy living, riverboat gambling, and the courtly life.

However, the civil war brought the city's high life to an abrupt end. The Union occupied New Orleans, outraging its citizens, and troops destroyed most of the surrounding plantations, cutting off its source of wealth.

When the Union troops left in 1877, Confederates resumed full political, civil, and economic power. "Separate but equal" mandates were firmly established to segregate black and white citizens, racial tensions heightened, and crime, prostitution, and corruption were rampant. In an attempt to control the lawlessness, city alderman Sidney Story sponsored a bill in 1897 that legalized prostitution within a thirty-eight block area, eventually to be known as Storyville. Here, in "sporting clubs," a new style of improvisational music called jazz was fostered along with an extraordinary culture of vice that lasted until the Department of the Navy closed it down in 1917.

World Wars I and II helped to temporarily boost the economy of the city, pumping money into the shipyards. The city has continued to struggle with racial tensions, crime, and corruption. However, it has never lost its reputation as a city of surpassing beauty complete with acres of wrought iron, gaily lit streets, and exquisite garden retreats, and courtyards. Most importantly, it continues to draw people who come for its renowned cuisine and musical culture, and, once a year, the spectacle of the Mardi Gras revelry.

OAK GROWN RUINS OF DE LA RONDE MANSION, NEW ORLEANS, LA.—149

GENERAL PAKENHAM'S HEADQUARTERS—1815

JACKSON STATUE, NEW ORLEANS, LA.—43

THE UNION MUST AND SHALL BE PRESERVED

GENERAL PACKENHAM'S HEADQUARTERS, NEW ORLEANS, LA.   6

Circa 1940s; $1-2

Circa 1920s; $3-5

The Jackson Statue was erected in 1846 by order of General Benjamin "Beast" Butler who occupied the city after the Civil War. His orders were carried out in the inscription at the granite base under the 20,000-pound figures, which reads "The Union must and shall be preserved."

Dated 1940s; $2-4

General Andrew Jackson and his ragtag troops defeated the British troops in the battle of New Orleans, fought on the plains of Chalmete near this site. The European Veterans' leader, General Edward Pakenham, was mortally wounded in the battle, and carried to this home a few miles south of the city, where he died of his wounds. The ruins of the DeLaRonde Plantation continue as a popular tourist destination, testament to the decisive end of the War of 1812.

The Pakenham Oaks, New Orleans, La.

Circa 1940s; $1-3

CHALMETTE MONUMENT, NEW ORLEANS.

E. O. KROPP PUBL., MILWAUKEE. NO 1212.

Circa 1900-07; $7

13536 CHALMETTE OAKS AND MONUMENT, NEW ORLEANS, LA. COPR. DETROIT. PUBLISHING CO.

The Chalmette National Memorial Monument was commissioned by the state in 1855 and completed with funds appropriated by the U.S. Congress in 1908 to commemorate General Andrew Jackson's defeat of the British.

Cancelled 1907-15; $8

The Washington Artillery commemorates the oldest field artillery battalion outside the original thirteen colonies, and the oldest militia unit from Louisiana. It participated in over 60 major engagements during the civil war, and in 1880 the Washington Artillery Benevolent Association raised funds to erect a monument to members who sacrificed their lives in the Civil War.

WASHINGTON ARTILLERY MONUMENT, GREENWOOD CEMETERY, NEW ORLEANS, LA.

Dated 1911; $4-6

10277. LEE MONUMENT, NEW ORLEANS, LA. 106 FEET HIGH AND COST $40,000.

COPYRIGHT 1906 BY DETROIT PUBLISHING CO.

A statue was raised to Confederate General Robert E. Lee and a public circle, Tivoli Circle, renamed, in 1883.

Circa 1900-07; $8

7

Crescent City

Bird's-eye view of Crescent City.

Circa 1907-15; $8-10

Aerial View, New Orleans, La. showing Bends in Mississippi River

The Bayou State

A bayou is a small, secondary river that feeds into larger bodies of water. Often marshy and slow moving, the state's nickname characterizes one aspect of life along the Mississippi. The city's history hasn't always revolved around its easy pace of life, however. Also nicknamed The Sugar State and The Child of the Mississippi, New Orleans served as a hub of commerce once its territorial masters in France and Spain eased up and allowed exportation to ports far and wide. Prior to the Civil War, New Orleans was the second most important port in the United States, and the sixth largest city.

From the back: "The winding path of the Mississippi River at New Orleans and the huge crescent, from which the city gets its title as "The Crescent City," are here clearly shown. The river continues on its sinuous journey to the Gulf of Mexico, 107 miles below the city."

Cancelled 1940s; $3-5

MISSISSIPPI RIVER CRESCENT, NEW ORLEANS, LA.—30

Two aerial views of New Orleans illustrate the city's nickname "The Crescent City." In passing, the river flows in all four compass directions within the city before heading off toward the Gulf of Mexico 107 miles away. The back of one card includes a tag line: "America's Most Interesting City."

Circa 1940s; $3-5

7080. EVENING ON BAYOU ST. JOHN, NEW ORLEANS, LA.

Evening on Bayou St. John in New Orleans.

Circa 1900-07; $7-9

MOONLIGHT ON THE MISSISSIPPI RIVER, NEW ORLEANS, LA.

Steamships plied the Mississippi from 1812 until the Civil War, ferrying agricultural crops and passengers through this important commercial hub.

Circa 1920s; $4-6

Circa 1940; $3-5

Circa 1940; $3-4

Excursion Steamer on Mississippi River, en Route to New Orleans, La.

Skyline of New Orleans, La., and Federal Barge Line Entering her Berth

By the middle of the 20th century, New Orleans was the fourth largest city in terms of area, covering over 200 square miles. Still one of the leading export ports, its primary wares including sugar, bananas, bauxite, and molasses.

Circa 1940s; $4-6

ALL STEEL MISSISSIPPI RIVER FERRY "LEO B. BISSO," NEW ORLEANS, LA.—161

A mile and a half wide, fourteen ferries were engaged in the process of transporting people across the river in New Orleans when this card was produced. The journey took five minutes.

Circa 1940s; $5-6

PONTCHARTRAIN BRIDGE, 5 MILES OVER WATER, NEW ORLEANS, LA.—147

Circa 1940s; $3-5

Bridge across Lake Pontchartrain, New Orleans, La.
World's Longest Continuous Concrete Highway Bridge

A card postmarked 1931 reads "A fine example of modern progress in New Orleans is the demonstration of what is being done to improve highway connections in this part of the country. Looking over the new $5,500,000 Pontchartrain Bridge...is the longest of its kind in the country. The actual span, entirely of concrete, is more than 5 miles in length and offers a chance for a beautiful cool drive over the waters...It brings New Orleans subsequently closer to the North and East."

Cancelled 1920s; $4-5

HUEY P. LONG BRIDGE, ACROSS THE MISSISSIPPI, NEW ORLEANS, LA.—187

Circa 1940s; $3-4

The Huey P. Long Bridge across the Mississippi was conceived of and built by the same-named senator. Spanning 4.4 miles including its approaches, and towering 409 feet high, the bridge was built to allow 135 feet of vertical clearance for passing steamers. It cost $13 million and three years to build, becoming the longest free bridge in the United States. The bridge formed a juncture between two transcontinental highways, the Old Spanish Trail from the Atlantic to the Pacific and Jefferson Highway from the Gulf of Mexico to Canada.

The Huey P. Long Bridge, New Orleans, La. Connecting New Orleans, La. with the Great West

Circa 1940s; $3-4

MOONLIGHT ON LAKE PONCHARTRAIN, NEW ORLEANS, LA.

Moonlight on Lake Ponchartrain.

Circa 1920s; $3-5

A toll-free span over the Rigolets, connecting Lake Borgne and Lake Pontchartrain, with Fort Pike (1819) a restored State Park.

Circa 1940s; $1-3

FORT PIKE AND RIGOLETS BRIDGE,
NEW ORLEANS, LA.

14

SOUTHERN YACHT CLUB, NEW ORLEANS, LA.—123

The Southern Yacht Club, the largest of its kind in the United States, located at the mouth of the New Basin, West End, New Orleans on Lake Ponchartrain.

Circa 1940s; $4-6

U. S. GOVERNMENT LIGHTHOUSE AT WEST END AND SEAWALL ALONG LAKE PONTCHARTRAIN, NEW ORLEANS, LA.

The U.S. Government Lighthouse at the West End and Seawall along Lake Pontchartrain.

Cancelled 1940s; $4-6

15

PONTCHARTRAIN BEACH, NEW ORLEANS, LA.—59

Pontchartrain Beach and Amusement Park at the northern end of New Orleans, only a short distance from the heart of the city, provides an early and convenient resort for residents in search of salt-water bathing, fishing, yachting, rowing, and other amusements. Kiddieland was touted as one of the finest children's amusement centers in the country, and big kids enjoyed the Zephyr Roller Coaster on the "gay Midway."

Circa 1940s; $4-6

PONCHARTRAIN BEACH AND AMUSEMENT PARK, NEW ORLEANS, LA.

Circa 1940s; $4-6

AIRVIEW OF PONCHARTRAIN BEACH
NEW ORLEANS, LA.—35

Circa 1940s; $4-6

A ferry terminal viewed from the air.

Circa 1940s; $5-7

10273. SUNDAY ON THE LEVEE. NEW ORLEANS. LA.

Early images illustrate the levee on Canal Street.

copyright 1906; $8-10

THE LEVEE AT CANAL STREET, NEW ORLEANS.

5366. COPYRIGHT, 1900, BY DETROIT PHOTOGRAPHIC CO.

Circa 1900-07; $9-12

Loading Cotton at New Orleans, La.

The Public Cotton Warehouse at New Orleans had a storage capacity of 461,800 bales, making it the largest ship-side warehouse in the world. Here bales of cotton are loaded for export.

Circa 1940s; $5-7

ONE OF THE 200 STORAGE COMPARTMENTS.

PART OF COMPRESS ROOM.

By the mid 1830s, half a million bales of cotton were shipping from the port of New Orleans, making it the cotton capital of the world. Cotton raised on plantations throughout the south was cultivated, picked, and ginned all over the south, then exported to looms around the world. Images portray cotton in the warehouse and terminal, and stacked on the levee.

Circa 1920s; $9-12

Circa 1907-15; $10-12

5821 COTTON ON THE LEVEE, NEW ORLEANS, LA.

PUBLIC COTTON WAREHOUSE AND TERMINAL, NEW ORLEANS, LA.

Home of the Sugar Bowl

Improvements in the processing of sugar cane are attributable to two important figures from New Orleans. Norbert Rillieux, whose father was a French engineer and plantation farmer, his mother a slave, showed great promise and was sent to France to study engineering. Upon returning to his hometown, he set to work inventing a drastically improved system of sugar refinement. Rillieux's work improved the end product of beet and cane sugar, cut costs drastically, and helped save many lives by reducing the crude, back-breaking, and very dangerous work previously performed by plantation slaves. He patented his device in 1846, and its use quickly spread throughout sugar plantations in Louisiana, Mexico, and the West Indies. A chemist from the U.S. Department of Agriculture, Charles Brown, said that Rillieux had "created the greatest invention in the history of American Chemical Engineering."

Etienne de Boré, a Louisiana plantation owner of noble Norman descent, risked his financial resources to pioneer a process to granulize the sugar. His breakthrough converted cane juice to granules that were easily stored and shipped. As a consequence, he died a rich man, and many plantation owners in the area switched crops from cotton to sugar to cash in on profits that could be nearly double the rewards for raising fibers.

Following the Civil War, Louisiana was producing between twenty-five and fifty percent of all the sugar consumed in the United States.

NEW ORLEANS, La. Sugar Exchange.

Cancelled in 1909, this card depicts the New Orleans Sugar Exchange building on Bieuville Street, organized in 1883 and boasting more than 200 members who gathered to share information about crops and lobby with regard to sugar legislation in Congress. The sugar lobby remains as a powerful force in state politics.

Cancelled 1909; $6-8

Sugar Wharf.
New Orleans, La.

Barrels of refined sugar await export on the Sugar Wharf of New Orleans.

Circa 1900-07; $7-9

HARBOR VIEW,
AMERICA'S SECOND LARGEST SEAPORT,
NEW ORLEANS, LA.—94

The ships from the "great white banana fleet" of the United Fruit Company line up at the wharf in New Orleans, the world's great banana port, with an annual importation of approximately 20 million bunches. At the time this image was taken, New Orleans' wharves spread along nine miles of river frontage.

Circa 1940s; $4-6

21

Unloading Bananas, New Orleans, La.—60

More than 700 ships a year arrived in New Orleans in the mid-20th century, each loaded with 25,000 to 50,000 bunches of bananas. Here workers move bunches from the ships' holds to the refrigerator car on mechanical conveyors.

Cancelled 1946; $4-6

Plantations

The rugged frontiersmen who cleared the land and drained the swamps along the Mississippi, established indigo as the area's first cash crop. By the 1800s, farming was underway on large-scale operations, some of which were established on large Colonial land grants, others from small lots pieced together. Few were as large as myth, however. Most were self-sufficient, the slaves producing and manufacturing most of the food, livestock, clothing, and other necessary goods for the inhabitants, and the larger holdings would maintain their own skilled slave labor in the form of blacksmiths or carpenters. From New Orleans, plantations dominated the scenery along River Road, which winds its way upriver from the city along the banks of the Mississippi, west into the heart of Cajun country. The same road has drawn tourists since the turn of the century, who venture out to view the more than 600 remaining plantations preserved throughout the state. Many are open as museums for touring, others have been restored and converted to bed and breakfasts. But reality often disappoints.

Gone with the Wind helped establish the Plantation Home of the South as romantic, gentrified homes, with slavery playing a backstage role. Architecturally, however, most of the remaining plantation homes are a disappointment to those raised on the Hollywood version – far smaller than homes being built by today's nouveau riche, and in many cases less grand. In the Creole tradition, plantation homes presented no pretensions in their outward structure, and the American style, though embellished with columns and porticos, seem somewhat cramped and humble in scale by today's standards.

"Four Oaks" plantation home.

Circa 1907-15, $6-8

From the back: "De La Ronde Oaks, Versailles Plantation, near New Orleans. Under these gigantic oaks, Gen. Jackson's men camped Dec. 23, 1814. Here de La Ronde, then Colonel, planned the Battle of New Orleans fought nearby on Jan. 1, 1815. This is the only large group of old live oaks in the world, 79 trees planted in 1783 by major Gen. Pierre Denis de La Ronde, scion of French nobility and distinguished in military activities."

Circa 1940s, $1-3

Slavery

The first slaves arrived in New Orleans in 1720, and the city soon became home to a large population of free Blacks working as artisans and operating their own business. Many came from Haiti during the 1791-1808 Haitian Revolution. By the mid 1800s, an estimated 13,000 blacks, slaves and free, were living in the city. Slaves made up almost half of the state's population, though nearly three-fifths of them lived outside the city, working the plantations.

Culturally, slaves brought with them an oral tradition of storytelling, voodoo practices, and chants and music that helped to spawn jazz and blues, believed by many to be the first indigenous music forms of the new nation.

The lives of slaves in the region was inextricably intertwined with that of the great plantations that fed New Orleans with exportable cotton and other agricultural goods. In turn, the city supplied plantation owners with freshly imported labor, whether fresh from Africa, or as stolen pirate booty from plundered merchant ships and port towns.

The nation's largest slave revolt took place just outside the city, in 1811. A group of slaves launched an attack upriver, led by a Saint-Domingue slave named Charles Deslondes. They marched down River Road toward the city, killing two whites, burning plantations and crops, and capturing ammunition. The revolt was suppressed, with sixty-six slaves killed and others captured and tried. Twenty-one slaves who faced trial were sentenced to death — shot and decapitated, with their heads displayed on pikes along the River Road to serve as warnings to other potential rebels.

10295. OLD SLAVE BLOCK, ST. LOUIS HOTEL, NEW ORLEANS, LA.

The Old Slave Block in the rotunda of the St. Louis Hotel. First built in 1835 at the astronomical cost of $1,500,000, the site was destroyed by fire in 1841.

Copyright 1906 by Detroit Publishing Co.; $6-8

Auctioneers of the city frequently used this site when they had slaves to sell, right up until the advent of the Civil War.

Copyright 1908 by C.B. Mason, New Orleans Publisher; $6-8

SLAVE BLOCK, IN OLD HOTEL ROYAL, NEW ORLEANS, LA.

Following a great fire that destroyed "the Old Slave Block," the site became home to Aunt Sally's Original Creole Pralines.

Circa 1940s; $10-12

Site of the Old Slave Block, corner of Royal and St. Louis Streets, New Orleans, La. — D-1

A LOUISIANA RICE FIELD.

Swamp and marshlands along the river delta was ideal for rice production.

Circa 1907-15, $4-6

GATHERING THE SEASONS CROP, SCENE IN AN ORANGE GROVE, NEAR NEW ORLEANS, LA.

An orange grove near New Orleans.

Circa 1920s, $3-5

Banana Tree Showing Bud and Fruit,

New Orleans, La.   4A-H1235

From the back: "… in New Orleans, where banana trees are to be found in many residential yards and gardens.

The French Quarter

Vieux Carre

When the Americans came, following a hasty land deal called the Louisiana Purchase, they found an enclave of Creole people who greeted them with great suspicion, and some disdain. Creole refers to people born in New Orleans, of French or Spanish descent. In Mediterranean style, the heart of their homes centered around an enclosed courtyard. And, like the walls surrounding these private retreats, the Americans found little entry in the heart of the established culture.

Thus the French Quarter remained so. The Vieux Carré, as the French speaking inhabitants called it, still retains its old world flavor, the historic buildings and narrow streets creating a center of charm, beauty, and intimate scale, all contained within a square mile of this vast and busy city. This is where visitors come to sample the Creole cooking of the old city's inhabitants, or the spicier Cajun dishes of the surrounding countryside, while enjoying live jazz. So beautiful and compact are the Quarters' attractions, that many tourists never venture beyond its confines.

From the back: St. Ann Street named by Adrian de Pauger in honor of the patron saint of the House of Orleans. In the French Quarter, homes were built flush to the sidewalks, called banquettes, so the homes on one side of the street would benefit from the shade of those on the other. New Orleans has some of the widest, narrowest, shortest and longest streets in the world."

Cancelled 1942; $4-6

Views of Chartres Street in the Vieux Carre. From the back of one: "Chartres Street, upon which through more than two centuries the horses, carriages, automobiles and slaves of many generations have trodden, is one of the treats New Orleans offers visitors in such abundance."

Circa 1907-15; $6-8

In the French Quarter.

Copyright 1904 by the Rotograph Co.; $10-12

Circa 1940s; $4-6

NAPOLEON BONAPARTE HOUSE, NEW ORLEANS, LA.

The noted LaFitte band of pirates plotted a bold plan to rescue French Emperor Napoleon Bonaparte and bring him to this house in New Orleans.

Cancelled 1951; $3-5

Chartres Street View, Old French Quarters, Showing Napoleon House, New Orleans, La.

It's not called the French Quarter for nothing! The Napoleon House on Chartres Street was erected in the mid 1800s to serve as a refuge for the Emperor himself, who was to be brought from St. Helena by a rescue expedition organized under the leadership of Nicholas Girod. Bonaparte's death thwarted the plans. Two doors down is another house built for the same purpose.

Circa 1940s; $4-6

29

ROYAL STREET, VIEUX CARRE, NEW ORLEANS, LA.—74

From the back: "Royal Street, looking toward Canal Street, in the heart of the Vieux Carre or Old Quarter. Many famous antique stores are found in this street." Once nicknamed Governor's Roy, Rue Royale has been home to five governors and two state Supreme Court Justices.

Circa 1920s; $9-12

From the back: "Royal Street is known throughout the world for its curio dealers, perfume shops, and antique stores where one can find beautiful specimens of old furniture, jewelry, chinaware and ancient firearms. In the early Creole days, Rue Royal was the main street of the French City and along its narrow thoroughfare are clustered many historical buildings. Every block of Royal Street teems with interest. It is one of the most interesting streets because of the many old homes, priceless wrought-iron railings, quaint courtyards and lovely gardens."

Circa 1940s; $4-6

Royal Street in New Orleans' French Quarter

Royal Street from Canal, the main thoroughfare of the city.

Circa 1907-15; $9-12

Royal Street looking toward Canal.

Circa 1907-15; $9-12

LACEWORK IN IRON, ROYAL ST., NEW ORLEANS, LA.—63

WINDOW BALCONIES, 600 BLOCK ROYAL STREET, NEW ORLEANS, LA.

From the back: "The Vieux Carre … is replete with architectural oddities. At 600 Block Royal Street, with shops on the ground floor and living quarters above may be seen an example of the famous window balconies."

Circa 1940s; $3-5

Lacework in iron on Royal Street. "The delicate traceries in cast and wrought iron embroidered on many of the old buildings."

Circa 1940s; $3-5

The French Market

A New Orleans institution since 1791, the French Market has long been a must-see sight for any visitor to town. Even today the streets around the market are the busiest in the French Quarter, where throngs mill to savor the sights and smells of Creole specialties, like strings of fresh garlic and peppers.

Native Americans first employed the sites to sell baskets, beads, and filé (ground sassafras leaves used in gumbo). Later African American women joined them to hawk rice cakes, and German farmers journeyed downriver to sell their produce.

Still occupying a five-block area between St. Ann and Barracks streets, the market now mixes a blend of local produce and flea market merchandise.

INTERIOR, FRENCH MARKET, NEW ORLEANS, LA.—36

The French Market focused primarily on produce when this image was recorded. The "Halle des Boucherires," as it was known during the French regime, was a busy food trading center.

Circa 1920s; $7-9

At the turn of the century, the French Market was "the most remarkable and characteristic spot in New Orleans, as under its roof every language is spoken."

Cancelled 1910; $9-12

1-FRENCH MARKET, NEW ORLEANS, LA.

Images taken in progressive decades illustrate how trolley lines and cars gradually took over the cobblestone streets.

Cancelled 1922; $8-10

Circa 1920s; $8-10

French Market, New Orleans, La.

Circa 1940s; $4-6

The Morning Call Coffee Stand in the old French Market, for "Connoisseurs in the art of French Drip Coffee. Patronized by tourists and notables the world over. Established 1870."

Circa 1940s; $5-7

A radio tower, paved streets, and "modern cars" add to the color and emerging modernity around the French Market. The backs of these late 1940s postcards talk about the "ceaseless babel" of languages within a structure that preserves the basic Spanish Colonial and roman Gothic architectural characteristics of a new structure on the site of a market first erected in 1813.

Circa 1940; $5-7

Pirate's Alley, New Orleans, La.

Pirate's Alley extends for one block from Royal Street to Chartres Street. Pirates were marched down this street enroute to the Cabildo Jail. Also known as Old Orleans Alley, it separates the Cabildo from Old St. Louis Cathedral.

Circa 1940s; $3-5

Circa 1940s; $3-5

Carondelet Street in New Orleans.

Cancelled 1909; $9-12

Carondelet Street, New Orleans, La.

Margaret Gaffney Haugherty earned a reputation as the benefactor of the orphans of New Orleans, irregardless of race. A self-made woman, an orphan herself, as well as widow and bereaved mother, Haugherty made her fortune with a bakery. During her lifetime she helped to build three orphanages, and when she died she left every cent of her money to the seven orphanages of the city. Her humble personage was depicted by sculptor Alexander Doyle and a park named in her honor. In 1956 a highway ramp hid the statue. Neighbors lobbied for years to have it removed, finally prevailing in 1994. Efforts are underway to restore the statue and grounds.

Cancelled 1920s; $5-7

In a postcard Cancelled 1907, the statue is shown in front of the Female Orphan Asylum.

Cancelled 1907; $6-8

Margaret Statue. The first Statue erected to a Woman's Memory in the United States. New Orleans, La.

This is a woman that gave all her property to build this Orphan Asylum H. M. W.

The Little Theater

Enthusiastic theater lovers, calling themselves the Drawing Room Players, soon outgrew their private spaces and even a rented building. Founded in 1916, Le Petit Theatre du Vieux Carre soon required a new theater – built in 1922 by architect Richard Koch, who designed it in authentic Spanish Colonial style, complete with a courtyard. It was one of the pioneering projects that helped revive the French Quarter, which in the early 1920s had become a slum. Still recognized as one of the leading community theaters in the nation, Le Petit Theatre du Vieux Carre was reconstructed in 1963 to contain a professionally equipped theater, reception rooms, offices, dressing rooms, and a smaller theater.

Circa 1940s; $2-4

LITTLE THEATER COURTYARD, NEW ORLEANS, LA.—44

619 ST. PETER STREET

THE LITTLE THEATER, NEW ORLEANS, LA.

1A832

From the back: The Little Theater, with a membership of nearly 3,000, has a nation-wide reputation. It is located at 616 St. Peter Street and forms the center of the Art Colony, a prominent feature in the life of Old New Orleans.

Cancelled 1941, $6-8

COURTYARD, LITTLE THEATRE,
NEW ORLEANS, LA.

**From one of the backs: "The courtyard
is one of the most beautiful in the city."**

Circa 1940s; $1-3

Little Theatre Courtyard,
New Orleans, La.

Circa 1940s; $1-3

COURTYARD OF LITTLE THEATRE,
NEW ORLEANS, LA.   178

Circa 1940s; $2-4

Cancelled 1934; $6-8

Circa 1940s; $2-4

Circa 1940s; $1-3

Circa 1940s; $2-4

Once serving as the Banque de la Louisiane, founded in 1804 as the first financial institution in the new U.S. territory. Many have resided here, including the world famous chess player Paul Morphy. The Patio Royal restaurant enjoyed many years of popularity, where visitors enjoyed the chance to dine in a courtyard once enjoyed by its owner. The restaurant has been known as Brennan's since 1956, and is still enormously popular.

Dated 1919; $6-8

Cancelled 1931; $6-8

Circa 1930s; $6-8

Three views of the Courtyard of the Two Sisters at 613 Royal Street. Originally occupied by Sieur Etienne de Perier, royal governor of colonial Louisiana between 1726 and 1733, and later the Marquis de Vaudreuil, the colonial royal governor credited with turning the marshy site into a "petit Paris." Two Creole sisters – Emma and Bertha Camors opened a notions shop on the site, outfitting well-to-do women of the area. The site has passed through several restaurateurs, and continues as a popular dining destination.

THE COURT YARD, PAT O'BRIEN'S NEW ORLEANS, LOUISIANA

**Pat O'Brien's courtyard restaurant is still doing a brisk business at 718 St. Peter St.,
on the site of the first Spanish Theater in the United States, built in 1792.**

Circa 1940s; $2-4

COURT YARD, ADELINA PATTI HOUSE, NEW ORLEANS, LA.

Circa 1940s; $2-4

The Adelina Patti House at 631 Royal Street is one of the oldest homes in the French Quarter dating back to the early 1700s. Patti (1843-1919) was an American-born Italian soprano who toured the United States as a child prodigy.

Court Yard; Adelina Patti House
New Orleans, La.

Cancelled 1951; $2-4

Courtyard in the French Quarter,
New Orleans, La.

Circa 1940; $2-4

BRULATOUR COURTYARD, 520 ROYAL STREET, NEW ORLEANS, LA.

Circa 1940; $3-5

The Brulatour Courtyard at 520 Royal Street is one of the most painted and photographed courtyards in New Orleans, as it was home to the New Orleans Art League in the 1930s. Built in 1816 by Francois Seignouret. From 1948 to 1996, it was home to WDSU-TV, and many celebrity interviews took place here, and the open patio was often frequented by tourists.

Circa 1940; $3-5

GALLERY FRENCH QUARTER, NEW ORLEANS, LA.

A gallery in the French Quarter.

Circa 1920; $5-6

From the back: "The Old Quarter of New Orleans abounds in hidden beauties like that in the picture – one of the enclosed courts, flower-filled and secluded, and breathing the atmosphere of ancient romance for which New Orleans is so famous."

Circa 1920; $3-5

COURTYARD OF THE HOME OF MRS. M. E. M. DAVIS, NEW ORLEANS.

From the back: "The court yards of the 'Vieux Carre' or old quarter of New Orleans, constitute its greatest charm, unique inheritances from the Creole settlers of the old city. Many of them are filled with beautiful gardens which are usually just temptingly visible through arched driveways like that at the right of the picture."

Circa 1940s; $2-4

Courtyard of Mrs. M. E. M. Davis in New Orleans.

Copyright 1901; $5-7

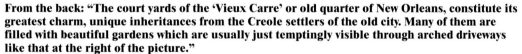

5813. COPYRIGHT, 1901, BY DETROIT PHOTOGRAPHIC CO.

11852 OLD FRENCH COURT YARD, NEW ORLEANS, LA.

Message penciled on the back in 1912: "I'll send you a whole collection from here... Mrs. Myers and I have been out in the touring car seeing some of these quaint places."

Cancelled 1912; $7-9

Still serving Creole cuisine at 819 Conti Street, this image of Broussard's Paradise Courtyard Restaurant was published in the 1930s.

Cancelled 1939; $4-6

BROUSSARD'S PARADISE COURTYARD RESTAURANT, NEW ORLEANS, LA.   63618

The courtyard of the Bosque House at 619 Chartres Street. The Good Friday fire originated here in 1788, in the house of Army treasurer Don Josc Vicente Nuòez and destroyed 856 buildings. Built in 1795 by Bartolome Bosque, a wealthy contractor, rebuilt here in 1795, and Suzette Bosque was born here and went on to become the third wife of Governor Claiborne.

Circa 1940s; $4-6

Courtyard, Governor Claiborne Home, New Orleans, La.

Fan Window in Governor Claiborne Home, New Orleans, La.

The home of Governor William C.C. Claiborne, who in 1804 became the first American Governor of the territory of New Orleans. A great diplomat, he overcame Creole suspicion of his outsider status, as he was initially appointed governor by Thomas Jefferson, and easily won the state's first gubernatorial election in 1812. The fan window and scenic courtyard at 628 Toulouse Street are considered excellent examples of French Quarter architecture. Today the site is home to shops and galleries.

Circa 1940s; $2-4 each

7021 OLD ABSINTHE HOUSE, NEW ORLEANS, LA.   ERECTED IN 1798

Possibly the most popular subject for a New Orleans postcard, this edifice's name was garnered via fiction. The name Madame John's Legacy stems from its role in a popular story "Tite Poulette" (1873) by George Washington Cable, in which the hero leaves this home on Dumaine Street to his quadroon mistress, who sells it, pockets the cash, and loses her money when the bank fails.

Dated 1919, $6-8

Madame John's Legacy is the oldest structure in the Mississippi Valley, built by Jean Pascal, a sea captain from Provence, France, who lived with his family until he was slain by the Natchez Indians in the massacre of 1729. In 1798 it served as headquarters to Jean Lafitte, the patriot pirate much celebrated in New Orleans fact and lore.

Circa 1920s, $6-8

OLD ABSINTHE HOUSE, NEW ORLEANS, LA.

STAIRWAY, OLD ABSINTHE HOUSE, NEW ORLEANS, LA.—53

Madam John's Legacy has also been called the Absinthe House, as it said that Frenchmen liked to gather here to sip the liquor.

Circa 1940s, $2-4

Madame John's Legacy
In the New Orleans' French Quarter

Madam John's Legacy became a boarding house in the late 19th Century. Today it is home to exhibits about the history of the home and its many notable residents in first floor galleries, as well as rotating contemporary art exhibits on the second floor.

Circa 1940, $2-4

51

Jean La Fitte's Blacksmith Shop in the Vieux Carré

Pirate turned patriot, Jean La Fitte is one of New Orlean's most colorful and celebrated characters. This blacksmith shop of his brother Pierre, erected in 1810 in the Vieux Carré, was said to be one of his favorite rendezvous sites, and served as his piratical headquarters.

Circa 1950s, $1-2

THE WARRINGTON HOUSE
(HAUNTED HOUSE).
1140 ROYAL STREET,
NEW ORLEANS, LA.

In a city rich in stories of voodoo, vampires, and specters, this home has served as its most haunted site. The story centers around the gruesome tale of a high-society mistress, Madame Delphine La Laurie, who came to town in 1832 with her family, only to flee two years later as a lynch mob gathered outside. The town learned of La Laurie's horrible torturing and killing of slaves in her attic after one of her servants set fire to the home, drawing firefighters into the residence. La Laurie escaped prosecution, but the tortured souls apparently remain at 1140 Royal Street.

Circa 1940; $4-6

FRENCH OPERA HOUSE BY NIGHT, NEW ORLEANS, LA.

Photographed shortly before it burnt down in 1919, the French Opera House was the center of artistic and social life in New Orleans. A pub now occupies the site on Bourbon Street and Toulouse. The New Orleans Opera Association, however, continues to operate as the oldest opera in North America, more than two centuries old.

Circa 1920s; $5-7

Antoine's Restaurant, 713 St. Louis St., New Orleans

Antoine's Restaurant at 713 St. Louis Street, established 1840.

Circa 1940; $2-4

COURTYARD OF GEN. P. G. T. BEAUREGARD HOUSE, CHARTRES STREET, NEW ORLEANS, LA.—211

Once the home of General P.G.T. Beauregard (1818-1893). Beauregard, a distinguished U.S. and Confederate general, was considered the greatest soldier born in New Orleans. The Beuregard-Keyes House is located at 1113 Chartres Street. It is also named for author Frances Parkinson Keyes, who wrote many of her books here including *Dinner at Antoine's*, and *Blue Camelia*.

Circa 1940; $2-4

Legendary Ironwork

The French District is notable for the beauty of its wrought iron, draped like lace over much of the architecture. The famed courtyards and gardens, most elusively secluded from view, are also part of the appeal of this beautiful city. Nearby, more gardens are on view in what is called the Garden District.

ORNAMENTAL IRON (CORN DESIGN) FENCE, 915 ROYAL ST., NEW ORLEANS, LA.—124

The Corn Fence,
915 Royal St., New Orleans, La.

The cornstalk and morning-glory motif fence around 915 Royal Street has been drawing tourists since the time it was cast in iron, sometime around the year 1850, by the prestigious Philadelphia company, Wood & Perot. The Victorian home within is now known as the Cornstalk Fence Hotel.

Left: Circa 1940; $2-6

Above: Circa 1940s; $1-3

Right: Circa 1940s; $1-3

Lacework in Iron
in Old New Orleans, La.

From the back: "These delicate lacework patterns in wrought and cast iron...give this quarter of New Orleans its atmosphere of Old France and Old Spain.

Circa 1940s; $3-5

LACEWORK IN IRON,
FRENCH QUARTER, NEW ORLEANS

An intricate iron balcony frames a view of the Old St. Louis Cathedral.

Circa 1940s; $3-5

FAMOUS LACE GRILLWORK, NEW ORLEANS, LA. — 217

LACEWORK IN IRON, ROYAL ST., NEW ORLEANS, LA.—63

An old house at St. Peter and Royal streets.

Circa 1940s; $2-4

From the back: "One can see much hand-hammered wrought iron-work, beaten by Negro slaves into its present designs."

Circa 1940s; $2-4

View of the Cabildo and St. Louis Cathedral from a lacework balcony.

Circa 1940s; $2-4

The iron gates of the Cabildo.

Circa 1920s; $2-4

Spanish Arms Patio, New Orleans, La. 10

The Spanish Arms Patio at 616 Royal Street. "In by gone Creole Days, famous beauties passed through these 'Wishing Gates' on their way to the large reception rooms above."

Cancelled 1946; $2-4

Jackson Square

Still a central meeting place, Jackson Square was first named the Place d'Armes in the early French colony, a muddy field where troops drilled, criminals did penance in the stocks or were executed in accordance with their crimes.

By the early 1800s, the most important complex of buildings was set up here for the early colony, with the Cabildo, the St. Louis Cathedral, and the Presbytère serving the administrative, spiritual, and judicial centers, respectively.

The site was renamed for Andrew Jackson after his defeat of the British in the 1815 Battle of New Orleans. Years later, in 1848, Baroness Pontalba paid for its beautification, laying out the gardens and pathways that distinguish it today. Today it sits in the heart of the business district, and on nice days artists exhibit their works along the iron fence that frames the radial pattern of walkways, and tarot card readers, jazz musicians, and entertainers work for spare change throughout the square.

A very early photographic view of the square.

Copyright 1903, Detroit Photographic Co.; $4-6

This monument to General Jackson was constructed by Clark Mills at a cost of $30,000. It was officially defaced by Union General Benjamin "Beast" Butler with an inscription at the base reading "The union must and shall be preserved."

Copyright 1900, Detroit Photographic Co.; $5-7

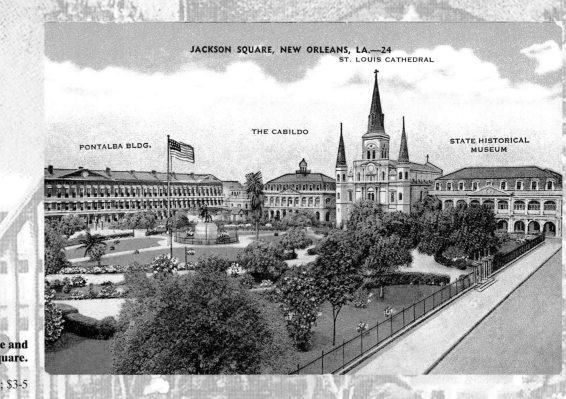

JACKSON SQUARE, NEW ORLEANS, LA.—24

ST. LOUIS CATHEDRAL

PONTALBA BLDG.   THE CABILDO   STATE HISTORICAL MUSEUM

Two mid-century cards identify the distinctive and important buildings that face Jackson Square.

Circa 1940s; $3-5

ST. LOUIS CATHEDRAL

CABILDO   STATE HISTORICAL MUSEUM   JACKSON MONUMENT   PONTALBA APARTMENTS

Jackson Square, New Orleans, La.

JACKSON SQUARE AND CABILDO, NEW ORLEANS, LA.

1A833

The St. Louis Cathedral was erected in 1718 by Don Almonaster y Roxas, and rebuilt in 1720 and 1794.

Circa 1920s; $4-6

View of the Cabildo
and St. Louis Cathedral
From a Lacework Balcony
New Orleans, La.

24

PONTALBA BUILDING, JACKSON SQUARE, IN THE OLD FRENCH QUARTER, NEW ORLEANS, LA.—92

The Pontalba Buildings on Jackson Square were built by the Baroness Micaela Almonester de Pontalba in 1848, boast some of the finest cast iron in the French Quarter and are part and parcel of the Baroness's contribution in revitalizing the quarter in the mid-1800s. Their design is based on apartment buildings she observed in Paris, and were considered the best and largest apartments of their day. The Baroness has a colorful story, involving her marriage to a distant cousin that took her from Louisiana to Paris, and a father-in-law who attempted to murder her when she refused to sign over her entire estate.

Circa 1940s; $2-4

**View of St. Louis Cathedral and the Cabildo
from a lacework balcony.**

Circa 1940s; $2-4

The Cabildo

The "Old Spanish Court" building was commissioned and built in 1795 by Don Almonaster Y. Roxas, who gave it to the city. The transfer of Louisiana from Spain to France and from France to the United States took place here in 1803. The Marquis de Lafayette lived here as a guest of the city in 1825. It served as a capitol for the legislative assembly of the Spanish colonial government, and subsequently as City Hall. It housed the Supreme Court and a prison from 1853 to 1911, and then became home to the Louisiana Historical Museum. A fire severely damaged the building in 1988, and it was closed for five years of extensive restoration. Today, exhibits within thoroughly and entertainingly trace the state's history.

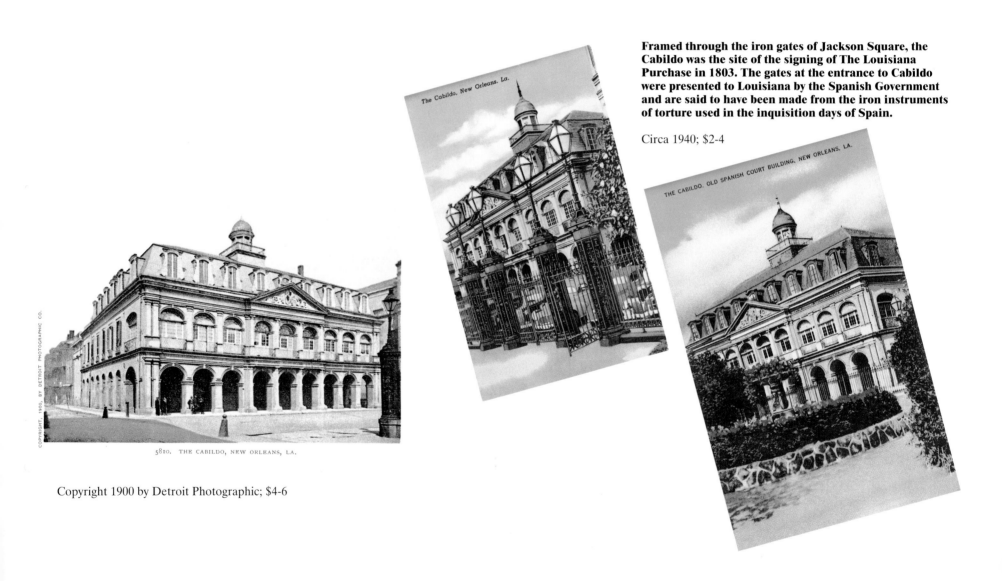

Framed through the iron gates of Jackson Square, the Cabildo was the site of the signing of The Louisiana Purchase in 1803. The gates at the entrance to Cabildo were presented to Louisiana by the Spanish Government and are said to have been made from the iron instruments of torture used in the inquisition days of Spain.

Circa 1940; $2-4

5810. THE CABILDO, NEW ORLEANS, LA.

Copyright 1900 by Detroit Photographic; $4-6

Stairway in the Cabildo,
New Orleans, La.

Stairway in the Cabildo, New Orleans, La.

Two views of a stairway within the Cabildo exhibit different eras of décor.

Circa 1940; $2-4

COURTYARD AND PRISON ROOMS IN THE CABILDO, NEW ORLEANS, LA.—151

Courtyard and Prison Rooms in the Cabildo, New Orleans, La.

Various angles explore the courtyard and prison rooms in the Cabildo. Here the Pirate Lafitte was incarcerated after his capture by the Americans. Later he helped General Jackson defeat the British, and became a local hero, earning a pardon from the United States Congress.

Circa 1940; $2-4

PHOTO BY "BILL" LEEPER   *Courtyard and Prison Rooms in the Cabildo, New Orleans, La.*

Business District

AIR VIEW OF NEW ORLEANS — THE MODERN METROPOLIS

An aerial view of Canal Street, on one side the French Quarter, on the other the business and financial district of the South's greatest city, and one of the world's great ports.

Circa 1940s; $4-6

Canal Street, the Broadway of New Orleans, La., showing Monoplane flying over street.

**Canal Street, "The Broadway of New Orleans,"
showing a monoplane flying overhead.**

Circa 1907-15; $10-12

Canal Street.

Copyright 1903; $10-12

7025. CANAL STREET NEW ORLEANS, LA.

From the back: "Canal Street, which takes its name from the fact that years ago an open drainage canal, now covered, ran down the center of the street, is perhaps the widest 'Main Street' in the United States. Its width – 171 feet – has made it famous. It is the dividing line between Old and New Orleans. It is famous the world over as the commercial and carnival center of New Orleans."

Cancelled 1948; $5-7

Canal Street, New Orleans, La.

PHOTO BY RAY CRESSON

From the back: "Canal Street …recently rebuilt at a cost of $3,500,000 … has sidewalks of terrazzo marble."

Circa 1920s; $8-10

CANAL STREET AT NIGHT, NEW ORLEANS, LA.—78

Canal Street and the ever-growing skyline of the "South's Greatest City"

Circa 1940s; $4-6

Canal Street is "lined with great department stores and smart specialty shops."

Circa 1940s; $4-6

Circa 1940s; $4-6

10284. ITALIAN HEADQUARTERS. MADISON STREET. NEW ORLEANS. LA.

**Italian Headquarters on Madison Street.
Begue's Exchange on the corner.**

Copyright 1906; $10-12

Copyright 1903; $6-8

COPYRIGHT, 1903, BY DETROIT PHOTOGRAPHIC CO.

8382. BEGUE'S EXCHANGE. NEW ORLEANS. LA.

COPYRIGHT, 1903, BY DETROIT PHOTOGRAPHIC CO.

ST. CHARLES STREET LOOKING NORTH.

(HIGH BUILDING WHITNEY CENTRAL BANK) NEW ORLEANS, LA

The Whitney Central Bank looms over Charles Street looking north.

Circa 1920s; $10-12

The U.S. Customs House, extending 340 feet along Canal Street is considered the most important Federal-style building in the South. Completed in 1881, it was designed by Alexander Thompson Wood. Over the years, the building has served as the post office, an armory, and a Union prison.

Circa 1920s; $4-6

U. S. CUSTOM HOUSE, NEW ORLEANS, LA.

New Masonic Temple, New Orleans, La.—135

11238. UNION STATION PARK. NEW ORLEANS, LA.

Union Station Park.

Copyright 1906 by Detroit Publishing Co. $4-6

A Scenic Spot in the Heart of the Business Section, New Orleans, La.

The New Masonic Temple, on the corner of Perdido and St. Charles Streets, was considered New Orleans most beautiful, modern office building when it was completed in 1927, at a cost of $2 million. Today it serves as the Hotel Monaco.

Circa 1920; $4-6

From the back: "One of the noteworthy characteristics of New Orleans is the semi-tropical appearance of its many parks. Here in the heart of the business section with luxuriant palms, azaleas, etc. affords a resting place for many tourists. The building in center background is the Southern Railway terminal."

Circa 1940s; $4-6

74

Lafayette Square

By the turn of the 20th Century, Lafayette Square was the center of state and national government in New Orleans, home to the United States District Court, U.S. Circuit Court of appeals, Weather Bureau, Secret Service, District Attorney, and other departments of Government service.

City Hall on a postcard dated 1906.

Circa 1900-07, $6-8

City Hall and Lafayette Place, New Orleans, from a very early post card, Cancelled in 1906.

Circa 1900-07, $6-8

The new Post Office facing Lafayette Square.

Cancelled 1919, $4-6

The new Post Office facing Lafayette Square.

Circa 1940s, $2-4

United States Post Office, New Orleans, La.

View from Lafayette Square. From the back: The skyscrapers of the Commercial center of New Orleans, the number of which is increased every month, for a peculiarly intriguing contrast with the century and a half old one and two-story brick and stucco structures of the old city.

Circa 1920s, $6-8

VIEW FROM LAFAYETTE SQUARE, NEW ORLEANS, LA.

LAFAYETTE SQUARE, SHOWING POST OFFICE, NEW ORLEANS, LA.—96

Lafayette Square showing the Post Office, City Hall, the Times-Picayune Building, and the First Presbyterian Church. In the Square are the Clay Monument, McDonogh and Franklin Statues.

Cancelled 1941, $2-4

77

Lee Circle, Showing Library and Shriners Temple, New Orleans, La.

First named Tivoli Circle, this site was renamed Lee Circle in 1883 after an enormous monument to Confederate General Robert E. Lee was erected. Home to the Public Library (a three-story brick building) and the Bienville Hotel (eight-story brick building) at the time these images were taken. More than 100 feet in height, the Robert E. Lee statue was created by sculptor Alexander Doyle at a cost of $40,000.

Circa 1940, $2-4

Circa 1940s, $2-4

ROBT. E. LEE CIRCLE, NEW ORLEANS, LA.—82

78

JOHN MCDONOGH MONUMENT,
NEW ORLEANS, LA.—42

John McDonogh's juicy story involves a great romantic disappointment, following which he became a recluse and, upon his death in 1850, he left his considerable fortune to the cause of education in New Orleans – enough to fund the construction of 32 public schools. His monument was built in Lafayette Square with dimes raised by grateful school children. For many years, a May festivity involved the contribution of flowers at the foot of his memorial by school children.

Circa 1920s; $3-5

The Garden District

As American entrepreneurs streamed into the area following the Louisiana Purchase in 1803, they were snubbed by the Creoles of the French Quarter. Undaunted, they built their own district of opulent mansions in nearby Lafayette, an area eventually dubbed the Garden District and annexed to the city in 1852. Garden District tours are a popular tourist attraction today. Most tours begin with St. Charles Avenue.

ST. CHARLES AVENUE SHOWING GIGANTIC LIVE OAKS, NEW ORLEANS, LA.—175

From the back: "St. Charles Avenue, because of the abundance, variety, and sizes of its trees, is described by tourists as one of the most charming residential avenues in the country. The avenue is five miles long, and along both sides are the beautiful homes of the city's well-to-do."

Circa 1940s; $2-4

Palms on St. Charles Avenue, New Orleans, La.

Palms stretch 60 to 70 feet in height and garnish a stretch of St. Charles Avenue.

Circa 1920s; $3-5

RESIDENCE, ST. CHARLES AVE., NEW ORLEANS, LA.

Copyright 1907, by C. B. Mason

A residence along St. Charles Avenue, the opulence of which drew visitors and inspired postcards such as this from the turn of the century.

Cancelled 1909; $6-8

The Public Library on St. Charles Avenue at Lee Circle. From the back: "It contains in excess of 200,000 volumes. Circulation approximately 750,000 volumes annually."

Circa 1920s; $4-6

Public Library, New Orleans, La.—117

THE TOURO--SHAKESPEARE HOME, NEW ORLEANS, LA.

The Touro-Shakespieare Home for the aged, one block from St. Charles Avenue on Arabella Street.

Circa 1920s; $4-6

F. B. WILLIAMS HOME (MARGUERITE CLARK), 5120 ST. CHARLES AVE., NEW ORLEANS, LA.—121

Home of motion picture actress Marguerite Clark (Mrs. Harry P. Williams) at 5120 St. Charles Avenue. Clark was billed as "America's first sweetheart." "From the back: This home with a beautifully terraced lawn is one of the popular types in the tree-shaded residential section of New Orleans."

Circa 1920; $4-6

"A beautiful entrance in the Garden District of New Orleans."

Cancelled 1947; $2-4

A Beautiful Entrance in the Garden District of New Orleans, La.   16

BEAUTIFUL BANANA TREE IN A FLORAL SETTING, NEW ORLEANS, LA.—29

From the back: "Tropically colorful and a sight to which most citizens of the United States are unfamiliar, … in New Orleans banana trees are to be found in many residential yards and gardens, bearing large bunches of the fruit."

Circa 1940s; $1-3

A Beautiful Entrance in the Garden District of New Orleans, La.   16

A beautiful entrance in the Garden District of New Orleans.

Circa 1940s; $2-4

84

Audubon Park

In 1871, the city purchased land that had already been put to much public service – as a Confederate camp, a Union hospital, and activation site for the 9th Cavalry, also known as the Buffalo Soldiers, and finally as the site of the World's Industrial and Cotton Centennial Exposition of 1884, Louisiana's first world fair. The city's plans were for an urban park, and planning of the facility was entrusted to landscape architect John Charles Olmstead, whose family firm designed New York's Central Park.

The name, Audubon Park, was adopted in 1886 to honor artist/naturalist John James LaForrest Audubon, a free black man who painted many of his famed "Birds of America" in Louisiana. A 1914 State Act established the Audubon Commission to maintain and develop the park. An aviary built in 1916 launched plans were begun for a full-scale zoo, which was built and stocked with private donations – for instance, school children in the state pooled funds to purchase an elephant in 1924.

The scenic urban Audubon Park was built in swampland that formerly served as the sugar plantation and home of Etienne de Boré, New Orleans' first mayor and founder of the nation's first commercial sugar plantation.

Circa 1907-15; $2-4

An image of Washington Oak in the new Audubon Park, one of the earliest images of the new park established in New Orleans.

Copyright 1900; $3-5

WASHINGTON OAK, AUDUBON PARK, NEW ORLEANS. LA.

The same oak and bridge, a few years later. A similar card states that "'Grey-bearded monarchs of the forest' is what the poets call these great live oaks that are to be found in the parks of New Orleans. In summertime their wide spreading branches shade picnic grounds for thousands of happy children."

Circa 1907-15; $2-4

The famous Avenue of the Oak Trees, estimated to be a thousand years old, in Audubon Park. Later known as Lover's Lane, this shady, winding road, "rendered more mysterious by the fall of night, has for decades been the scene of romantic trysts. Strolling on foot was replaced by cozy carriages and this in turn gave way to low-hung coupes and roadsters, states a similar card published in the 1940s.

Circa 190-15; $2-4

FAMOUS AVENUE OF OAK TREES (1000 YEARS OLD.) AUDUBON PARK, NEW ORLEANS, LA.

FLYING CAGE, AUDUBON PARK, NEW ORLEANS, LA.—191

The Flying Cage built in 1916 in Audubon Park proved so popular that plans were soon underway for a full-scale park. Within, pelicans, cormorants, night herons, European stork, and various American species of geese, ducks, and gulls were displayed.

Circa 1940s; $3-5

Audubon Park and View of Zoo, New Orleans, La.

A view of the zoo in Audubon Park.

Circa 1940s; $2-4

From the back: "Here is a profusion of luxuriant red roses of every shade and size. Of botanical interest is a richly red hybrid rose developed by the superintendent of the Park, Frank E. Neelis."

Circa 1940s; $2-4

From the back: "Over a half million dollars have been expended in Audubon Park to provide every conceivable phase of recreational activity. Of the countless recreational facilities constructed, one of the most popular is the W. B. Riley Wading Pool, a delight to the youngsters."

Cancelled 1945; $2-4

Audubon Park looking toward the clubhouse.

Circa 1940s; $2-4

City Park

Originally the Louis Allard plantation, at 1500 acres, City Park is one of the largest urban parks in the country. The original parcel of land was left to the city by philanthropist John McDonogh after his death in 1950. Innumerable entertainments and an incredible collection of historic oak trees are among the many amenities of this huge recreation area, extending from Bayou John to the Orleans canal.

A statue of Confederate General P. G. T. Beauregard stands at the entrance to City Park, mounted in 1915 on a granite base.

Circa 1920; $4-6

VIEW IN CITY PARK, NEW ORLEANS, LOUISIANA

A very early view of City Park.

Circa 1900-07; $4-6

NEW ORLEANS, La.   City Park Race Track.

Winter races were held for three years in a half-million dollar facility that was one of "the finest and most modern race tracks in the country," according to the back of this card. Opened in 1905, it shut down after only three years.

Cancelled 1907; $6-8

89

The Peristyle, City Park, New Orleans, La. 12964

No. 15. A PATHWAY IN CITY PARK. NEW ORLEANS, LA.

© C.B.M.

The Peristyle was built in 1907 for open-air dances.

Circa 1907-15; $6-8

From the back: "City Park contains 216 acres and was a part of Louis Allard's plantation, extending from Bayou St. John to the Orleans Canal."

Cancelled 1918; $2-4

In 1913 a Casino was opened to serve refreshments and a bandstand in front was dedicated on July 4th, 1917.

Cancelled 1920; $3-5

BAND STAND AND CASINO, CITY PARK, NEW ORLEANS, LA.

CITY PARK SCENE, NEW ORLEANS, LA.—41

From the back: "In City park are handsome conservatories, golf links and polo field, while rowboats may be obtained for a little excursion on the lake. Comprises some 263 acres on the banks of Bayou St. John – one of nature's beauty spots.

Cancelled 1935; $2-4

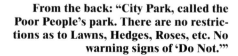

Beautiful Stone Bridge in City Park, New Orleans, La.

From the back: "City Park, called the Poor People's park. There are no restrictions as to Lawns, Hedges, Roses, etc. No warning signs of 'Do Not.'"

Circa 1920; $2-4

TROPICAL GARDENS,
CITY PARK,
NEW ORLEANS, LA.—220

From the back: "The park is a splendid example of landscape gardening art, with a lake, radiating lagoons, and wooded walks, golf links and a polo field; the grove of live oaks is one of the finest known." The lagoons and many other features of the park were completed as part of a WPA project during the Great Depression.

Circa 1940s; $1-3

Suicide Oak, City Park, New Orleans, La.

From the back: "This tree has been particularly attractive to persons who wish to depart this life … many persons have been found under this oak with an empty vial, or gun by their side, hence its cognomen, Suicide Oak." It is related that, in a 12-year span, 16 men committed suicide under these branches.

Circa 1940s; $1-3

Circa 1920; $2-4

NEW ORLEANS, La. Dueling Oaks. City Park

My dear Anna, Here we all well and safe I hope you are the same, writ when you can, as I shall do you. Love from all Louis Armstrong 1240 St Charles Ave. New Orleans. La.

These oaks were for those who wished to take others' lives. The Old Dueling Oaks in City park got their name from the legend and history of important men settling their differences here. Among them, Micaja Lewis, secretary to Governor Claiborne, was killed here in 1804. Emile LaSere, a member of Congress from New Orleans, fought eighteen duels in the course of his life. And U.S. Senator Waggaman was killed under the oaks. On one Sunday in 1837, ten duels were fought here. One card shows an artistic interpretation of the De Lissue Le Boisque duel in 1841. The other scenes illustrate the popularity of this spot among visitors to City Park.

Cancelled 1900-07 $4-6

OLD DUELLING GROUNDS IN CITY PARK, NEW ORLEANS, LA.—69

SHOWING DE LISSUE LE BOISQUE DUEL IN 1841

Circa 1920; $3-5

The Delgado Art Museum, donated by the late Isaac Delgado, opened in 1911. It was renamed in the 1970s as the New Orleans Museum of Art.

Circa 1920s; $3-5

Cities of the Dead

New Orleans cemeteries are unforgettable. Something of a cross between the famous tombs of Père Lachaise Cemetery in Paris, and the shrines of Mexico, it's above-ground tombs are must-see attractions, and a unique lesson in the history and culture of the city.

The above-ground tombs owe their existence to the climate – waterlogged soil rarely keeps its secrets. Two kinds of vaults are found in the cemeteries of New Orleans, family vaults and "oven crypts." Resembling ovens, the oven crypts use solar heat to help reduce the contents of each vault to bone within a few years time. The dry bones are then pushed into a communal pit in the back, and room made for the next occupant. Thus many names are engraved on these vaults, and room is always being made for yet another.

Ann Rice helped popularize these cemeteries, featuring them in her popular vampire tales. However, long before the author's fans started flocking to these sites, the graveyards were drawing tourists, as the following postcards illustrate.

75—Old St. Louis Cemetery, New Orleans, La.

St. Louis Cemetery

5819 OLD VAULTS IN ST. LOUIS CEMETERY, NEW ORLEANS, LA.

At one point the Old Saint Louis Cemetery fell into such disrepair that visitors might stumble across bones, as well as broken monuments. Restoration work has helped to restore many of the ruins.

Circa 1907-15; $6-8

The first cemetery, St. Louis No. 1 (1789), and St. Louis No. 2 (1823) served the original needs of the French Quarter residents.

Cancelled 1908; $6-8

OLD ST. LOUIS CEMETERY, NEW ORLEANS, LA. — 15

From the back: "The most interesting of New Orleans historical burial places, the St. Louis Cemetery No. 1 – there are three – has been in use for 175 years, with some of the inscriptions still decipherable dated 1800. Here lies the bodies of Paul Morphy, the famous chess player; Gayarre, the historian; Etienne de Bore, who first made granulated sugar; Charles LaSalle, brother of the famous explorer."

Circa 1940; $2-4

Vaults of Old St. Louis Cemetery
New Orleans, La.

Oldest Cemetery, St. Louis No. 1, New Orleans, La.

From the back: "Vaults in St. Louis Cemetery, nearly all more than one hundred years old, decorated lavishly with flowers on All Saints' Day, November 1st, according to a colorful custom characteristic of New Orleans."

Cancelled 1953; $3-5

Circa 1940s; $3-5

Metairie Cemetery

Considered the most attractive of New Orleans cemeteries, this lush former race track is bejeweled with the elegant tombs of the city's bluebloods and tycoons. Burials have been taking place here since Charles T. Howard purchased the property in 1872.

Circa 1907-15; $6-8

From the back: "… in which are to be found the graves of many of the early French and Spanish settlers. Here also is the resting place of the famous pirate, Dominick You."

Circa 1940s; $3-5 each

METAIRIE CEMETERY, SHOWING FINE TOMBS, NEW ORLEANS, LA.

Metairie cemetery is notable for its statuary and magnificent tombs. The women strolling on the right illustrate the early popularity of visits to the area's notable cemeteries.

Circa 1920; $4-6

8385. METAIRIE CEMETERY, NEW ORLEANS, LA.

An early view of the tombs in Metairie Cemetery.

Copyright 1900 by the Detroit Photographic Co.; $7-9

VIEW IN METAIRIE CEMETERY, NEW ORLEANS, LA.—116

From the back: "Metairie Cemetery, once a race track, turned into a burial place, for revenge, by a blackballed applicant for membership in the Jockey Club (Charles T. Howard)."

Circa 1920; $4-6

COPR. DETROIT PUBLISHING CO.

10306   TOMB OF THE ARMY OF TENNESSEE, METAIRE CEMETERY, NEW ORLEANS, LA.

Circa 1907-15; $6-8

A tomb in which soldiers of the Army of Tennessee, including local Civil War hero General Beauregard, is topped by a statue of Albert Sidney Johnston.

Circa 1920s; $4-6

METAIRIE CEMETERY, NEW ORLEANS, LA.

2B596

Two views of the gateway to Metaire, "considered the most beautiful (cemetery) in America."

Circa 1940; $2-4

Circa 1940; $2-4

LAKE IN METAIRIE CEMETERY, NEW ORLEANS, LA.—115

A lake in the park-like Metaire Cemetery.

Dated 1947; $2-4

St. Roch's Chapel

7077 ST. ROCH'S CHAPEL, NEW ORLEANS, LA.

The Rev. Father Thevis prayed to St. Roch, patron saint of plague victims, to protect his flock during an 1867 epidemic in New Orleans. When the parish weathered the pestilence, he made good on his promise and built a chapel in 1871 to the saint.

Copyright 1903; $7-9

From the back: "It is here many thousands of persons have gone and made a novena to St. Roch, the patron of Health. Tapers placed there by those desiring the assistance of their patron are almost continually burning before the altar. On all four walls can be seen offerings of thanks laid there in gratitude for favors granted."

Circa 1907-15; $7-9

St. Roch's Chapel, New Orleans, La.

COPR. DETROIT PUBLISHING CO.

13529 ST. ROCH'S CHAPEL, NEW ORLEANS, LA.

St. Roch's Chapel and graveyard.

Circa 1907-15; $8-10

From the back: "Few who visit New Orleans fail to visit St. Roch's with its unusual above-ground burial niches, like pigeon holes in the wall that surrounds the ancient cemetery and its romantic Shrine in the center, with storied charm for bringing love to girls who pray therein after visiting nine churches."

Circa 1920; $6-8

ST. ROCH'S CHAPEL, NEW ORLEANS, LA.—12

Churches

At the time of the Louisiana Purchase in 1803, the French and Spanish population of New Orleans was predominantly Roman Catholic. The rich religious culture has helped to spawn its signature Mardi Gras carnival, and helped populate the city with a rich landscape punctuated by church steeples.

Beautiful murals were added to the church's interiors in 1892. The tombs of the Marignys lie beneath the floor in front of the altar. Bernard de Marigny (1788-1871) inherited millions as a young man, and squandered it all playing craps, a game he introduced to America.

Circa 1940s; $2-4

St. Louis Cathedral in Jackson Square was erected in 1718 by Don Almonaster y Rosas, a wealthy Spaniard, who donated it to the parish. Rebuilt in 1720, and again in 1794. The present building was built from plans drawn in 1849 by French-born architect Jacques N. B. de Pouilly.

Circa 1940s; $2-4

ST. LOUIS CATHEDRAL
JACKSON SQUARE
NEW ORLEANS, LA.—177

St. Anthony's Alley, for centuries a promenade of the priests of St. Louis Cathedral, was renamed for the beloved Spanish Capuchin Pere Antonia of Sedella, who served at the cathedral until his death in 1829.

Spanish Capuchin Pere Antonio of Sedella served from 1783 until his much-lamented death in 1829. Here lay the bones of old Don Almonster, and of the said Friar Antonio, for whom the people named Pere Antoine's Alley alongside the church.

Circa 1940s; $2-4

AERIAL VIEW OF URSULINE CONVENT, NEW ORLEANS, LA.

An aerial view of Ursuline Convent on Chartres St. The Sisters of Ursula established Catholic schools for African-American and Native American girls, and set up the first orphanage in Louisiana. The convent is now home to Catholic archives dating back to 1718. It is the oldest building of record in New Orleans and the entire Mississippi Valley.

Circa 1920s; $7-9

The Archbishopric. St. Louis Cathedral became home to the city's first bishop in 1793, and 60 years later New Orleans became an archbishopric, elevating the cathedral further. Today the church contains the remains of eight New Orleans bishops.

Dated 1919; $6-8

SACRED HEART CHURCH, CANAL AND SO. LOPIZ STREETS.

NEW ORLEANS, LA.

1:—St. Marks Community House

19307

corner of North Rampart and Governor Nichols Street, New Orleans, La.

Sacred Heart Church at 3200 Canal Street, built for a parish founded in 1879.

Circa 1920s; $6-8

From the back: **"St. Mark's Community House is one of the most complete plants of its kind in America. It includes church, free clinic, gymnasium, swimming pool, clubs for boys, girls, men, and women, apartments for staff workers, a Church of Nations maintained by M. E. Church, south."**

Cancelled 1928; $6-8

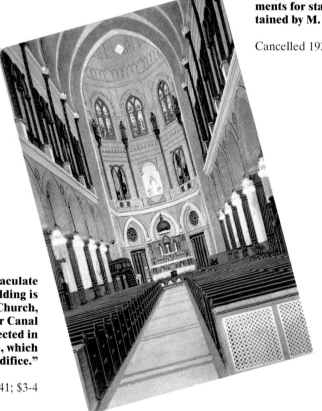

From the back: **"Church of the Immaculate Conception…This magnificent building is popularly known as the Jesuit Church, located on Baronnet Street near Canal Street. The original chapel was erected in 1848, a new church completed in 1857, which was replaced by the present modern edifice."**

Cancelled 1941; $3-4

Beginning in 1805, Christ Church became the first congregation to offer non-Roman Catholic services. Several impressive churches were built for the congregation. The one shown was designed in the late 1800s by New York architect Lawrence B. Valk for the corner of St. Charles Avenue and Sixth Street.

Copyright 1901 by Detroit Photographic; $6-8

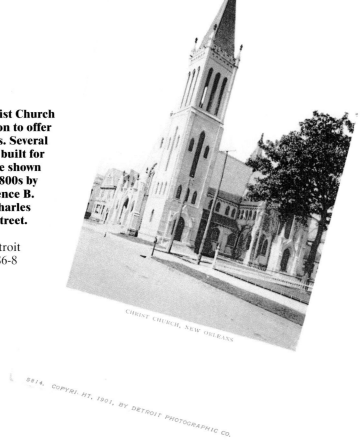

CHRIST CHURCH, NEW ORLEANS

5814. COPYRIGHT, 1901, BY DETROIT PHOTOGRAPHIC CO.

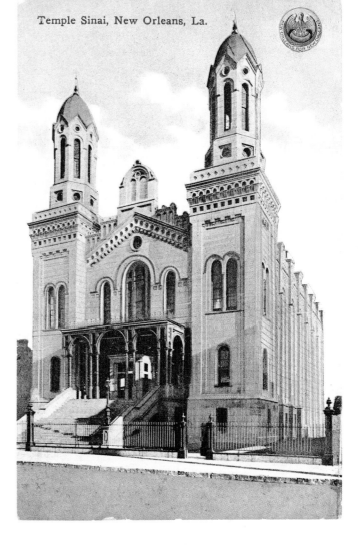

Temple Sinai, New Orleans, La.

Temple Sinai, on scenic St. Charles Avenue, was established in the late 1800s. The city has long had a Jewish population, though small in numbers, which nevertheless has been a dominant force in the fabric of the City.

Circa 1907-15; $6-8

Mardi Gras

Lent, beginning on Ash Wednesday, is observed by Catholics around the world with fasting and self-deprivation. In New Orleans, the days, and weeks, leading up to Lent more than make up for upcoming suffering.

Over the course of 250-plus years, the Mardi Gras carnival in New Orleans has become world-renowned for its largess and, in many instances, utter depravity. Today the excitement and revelry culminates on Bourboun Street on Fat Tuesday (Mardi Gras is French for Fat Tuesday). Through the years, a tradition of parades, balls, and widespread revelry has grown up, ranging from family events to liquor-drenched orgies – something for everyone.

A panoramic view of Canal Street. This "Trifold Post Card" was printed in Germany by Raphael Tuck & Sons, "Art publishers to their majesties the King and Queen" in England.

Copyright 1904; $25-30

Mardi Gras
Carnival.
New Orleans,
La.

Horse-drawn floats make their way through throngs of people on Canal Street.

Copyright 1907 by Detroit Publishing Co.; $10-12

The King Rex Pageant was created in 1872 to welcome the grand duke of Russia, Alexis Alexandrovich Romanov to town. The duke came with his love interest, actress Lydia Thompson, when she came to star in Bluebeard. Her burlesque tune, "If I Ever Cease to Love You," was played by all the floats in the parade that year, and is the official song of Mardi Gras.

Copyright 1907 by Detroit Publishing Co.; $10-15

10302. THE "REX" PAGEANT, MARDI GRAS DAY, NEW ORLEANS, L'A.

King Rex, Merry Monarch of Misrule, is presented with the key to the city in front of City Hall.

Copyright 1907 by Detroit Publishing Co.; $10-12

Circa 1940s; $7-9

Canal Street on Mardi Gras.

Cancelled 1907; $12-15

Canal Street. Mardi Gras.   New Orleans, La.

King's Float. Mardi Gras.   New Orleans, La.

The King's Float parades before packed balconies and makeshift viewing platforms.

Circa 1900-07; $12-15

From the back: "…Paper mache floats, depicting mythical, historic or phantastic theme, frolic, frolicking, masquerading, festive feelings, freely expressed without restraint, an outbreaking of the love of pleasure that exists in every normal human being."

Circa 1940s; $7-9

Aerial views of Canal Street on Mardi Gras. From the backs: "Canal Street is the country's widest business thoroughfare and one of the most beautiful and best lighted. It is lined with high class department stores and theaters." From another: "… it's new coat of terrazzo marble is entirely hidden beneath the feat of festive throngs gathered here from all the corners of America."

Circa 1920s; $7-9

Circa 1940s; $7-9

112

Circa 1940s; $7-9

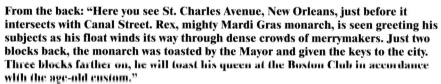

Canal Street During Mardi Gras, New Orleans, La.   13

From the back: "At New Orleans, the gayest of good times is Mardi Gras, the bacchanalia that ushers in the Lenten season, and every year brings hundreds of thousands of visitors to the city. On Mardi Gras (Shrove Tuesday) the entire city turns out for one of the Greatest Shows in America."

Circa 1940s; $7-8

From the back: "Here you see St. Charles Avenue, New Orleans, just before it intersects with Canal Street. Rex, mighty Mardi Gras monarch, is seen greeting his subjects as his float winds its way through dense crowds of merrymakers. Just two blocks back, the monarch was toasted by the Mayor and given the keys to the city. Three blocks farther on, he will toast his queen at the Boston Club in accordance with the age-old custom."

Cancelled 1938, $7-9

Carnival parades are hosted by krewes, clubs that were initially quite exclusive. The culmination of their annual event would be a ball in which a king and queen were chosen and or crowned, and the lavish and almost legendary parades they would launch.

Circa 1940s; $10-12

K5130 *King and Queen of The Many Carnival Balls staged Before Mardi Gras, New Orleans, La.*

ALLA, KING OF THE PORT ARRIVES, MARDI GRAS, NEW ORLEANS, LA.—170

From the back: "With his cohorts of the sea, King Alla of the West Bank has restored to New Orleans one of the high color spots which faded from the rainbow of the New Orleans Mardi Gras during the World War. At High Noon on the Monday preceding Ash Wednesday, King Alla arrives from 'somewhere around the Sargaso Sea' with an imposing marine pageant on the grand old man of the rivers and after landing parades around the West Bank and presides over a sumptuous Mardi Gras Ball."

Circa 1940s; $10-12

Beauty Under Mask,
Mardi Gras Time, New Orleans, La.

Revelers in costume are called "maskers," and the anonymity helps bring out the revel in everyone. From the back: "... music and dancing and noise and colorful atmosphere make a debutante's heart burn. Costumes as colorful as a painter's canvas and as numerous as ants give to New Orleans its characteristic aspect at Mardi Gras time."

Cancelled 1942; $10-12

Float in Mardi Gras Parade, New Orleans, La.

From the back: "New Orleans carnival ... is superior in pomp and gorgeousness to any celebration of this kind anywhere in America or abroad. Mardi Gras dates back to 1827 and the floats first appeared in 1837."

Circa 1940s; $10-12

A Group of Maskers on Canal Street, Mardi Gras Day, New Orleans, La

Maskers on Canal Street sport blackface at a time when this was not considered politically inappropriate. Blacks were excluded from participation in the revelries for many years, and many traditional krewes quit parading when government regulations required that they integrate. The parade of King Zulu, a black krewe, is among the festival's most popular since its inception in 1906.

Circa 1940s, $10-12

Colorful Float in Mardi Gras Parade

From the back: "... add up the thousands of enthusiastic revelers and spectators lining the route of march and you have something of the 'Spirit of Mardi Gras.'"

Circa 1940s; $7-9

"Maskers" aboard a peanut float bear bags of "throws," gold coins, necklaces, and other trinkets that are tossed generously to the crowds.

Circa 1940s; $7-9

Mardi Gras on Float in Rex Parade Giving Favors to Crowds on Canal Street, New Orleans, La.

K5126

Maskers on Float of Rex Parade, Mardi Gras Day, New Orleans, La.

The tradition of giveaways or "throws" began in the 1880s, and has become part of the tradition of excess of Mardi Gras.

Circa 1940s; $7-9

Crowds Viewing Rex Parade

From the back: "King for a day, Rex, Merry Monarch of Misrule, again dons his royal robes and jewel studded scepter to rule a frenzied populace when the long awaited day arrives."

117

Mardi Gras Float from the Realms of Phantasy

From the back: "Momus, the Greek god of mockery and censure, is the first of the major processions, and is followed by Hermes, King Nor, Proteus, Rex and Comus. Mardi Gras day presents a spectacle of miles of glittering floats with thousands of people lining the streets."

Circa 1940s; $7-9

A Fantastic Mardi Gras Float

From the back: "… convey the male members of the various Carnival Krewes from their mysterious dens to the scene of the ball where the Queen and her maids await them."

Circa 1940s; $7-9

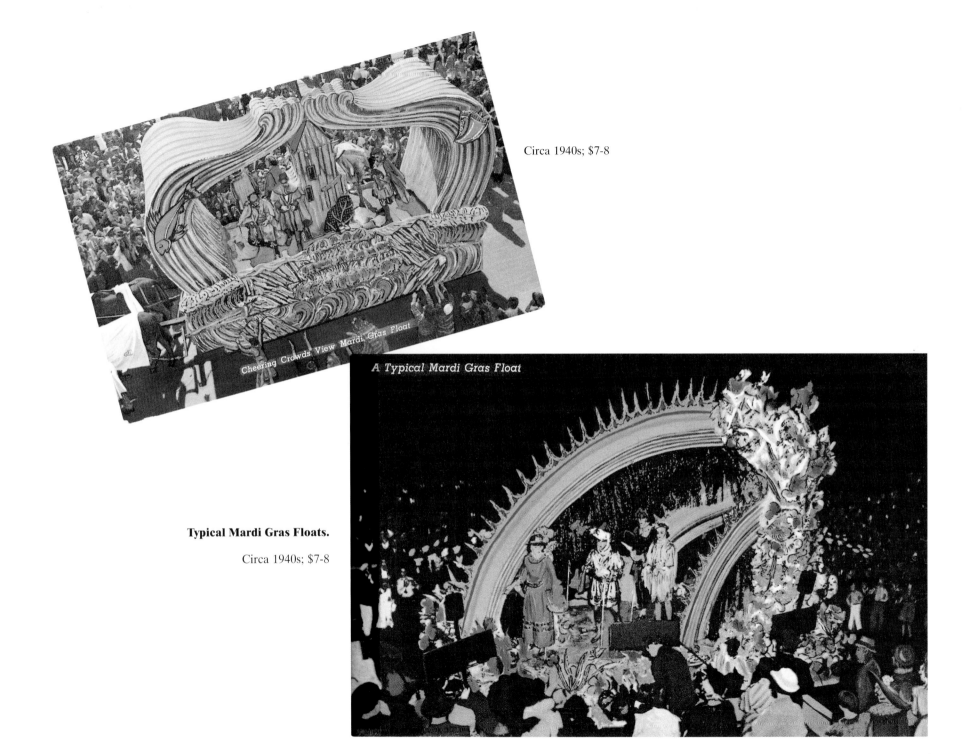

Circa 1940s; $7-8

Typical Mardi Gras Floats.

Circa 1940s; $7-8

From the back: "In the evening Rex is host at a royal ball and at eleven p.m. he and his queen leave to pay a royal call on the court of Comus."

Circa 1940s; $7-9

A Typical Mardi Gras Float

Circa 1940s; $7-9

Crowds Waving at Maskers on Floats of Rex Parade on Canal Street, Mardi Gras Day, New Orleans, La.

From the back: "This view represents the King meeting his Queen where he drinks a toast to his Queen of the traditional champagne, after which he wends his way through his fun-mad subjects and becomes what his heritage commands, King for a Day."

Cancelled 1946; $7-9

MARDI GRAS PARADE FLOAT, NEW ORLEANS, LA.—232

Elaborate floats in Carnival parades.

Circa 1940s; $7-9 each

Colleges and Universities

NOTRE DAME SEMINARY, NEW ORLEANS, LA.—34

In keeping with its Catholic heritage, New Orleans is home to Notre Dame, the major Seminary of the archdiocese of New Orleans. From the back: "… One of the most beautiful and majestic buildings in the city, is a monument to the zeal of Archbishop Shaw, whose residence is shown at the right. The property embraces ten squares, affording ample space for recreation and further development."

Circa 1940s; $2-4

TULANE UNIVERSITY, NEW ORLEANS.

5811. COPYRIGHT, 1900 BY DETROIT PHOTOGRAPHIC CO

Founded in 1834 as the university of Louisiana, Tulane University has become one of the South's foremost educational institutions.

Copyright 1900 by Detroit Photographic; $6-8

GIBSON HALL, TULANE UNIVERSITY, NEW ORLEANS, LA.—40

Cancelled 1941; $2-4

Givson Hall housed administrative offices of Tulane University. The campus borders Audubon Park.

Cancelled 1947; $2-4

Tulane University, New Orleans, La.

LOYOLA UNIVERSITY, NEW ORLEANS, LA.—104

Circa 1940s; $2-4

The Tudor Gothic tower of Loyola University overlooks Audubon Park. The Jesuit college adjoins Tulane University.

Circa 1940s; $2-4

LAGOON IN AUDUBON PARK, LOYOLA UNIVERSITY IN BACKGROUND, NEW ORLEANS, LA.—168

**Soulé College, "The South's Greatest School of Business,"
facing Lafayette Square. Alone on the landscape in 1909, it got
a new neighbor in the Neo-Classical form of a city hall by 1919.**

Cancelled 1909, $6-8

Valuing Postcards

The values shown in this book are provided as a guideline for collectors and dealers. The values are based upon rarity of the postcard views. Condition has not been factored in and should be considered when evaluating individual postcards.

A Short History of the Postcard in the United States

Historians divide postcards into eras that reflect the general style of postcard printed, as well as the photo and color techniques. More dating clues can be gleaned with an understanding of cancellations and postage, along with visual clues such as the style of dress and era of transportation pictured.

An abundance of vintage postcards and an endless variety of collecting subjects make this an attractive and addictive hobby. The abundance of old postcards owes to the enormous popularity that postcard collecting enjoyed in the early 1900s. Picture postcards of exceptional quality circulated the globe in the first years of the century, and postcards were arguably the greatest collectible hobby that the world has ever known. The U.S. Post Office figures for the fiscal year ending June 30, 1908, cite 677,777,798 postcards mailed, at a time when the total population of the U.S. was 88,700,000! World War I cut off the supply of exceptionally beautiful, high-quality cards from Germany, and ushered in an era of lesser-quality cards at the same time that telephones were replacing the need for written missives in casual communications. Nonetheless, the hobby survives, and in surprising strength for those new to the niche.

Pioneer Era (1893-1898)

Although there were earlier scattered issues, most pioneer cards in today's collections begin with the cards placed on sale at the Columbian Exposition in Chicago, Illinois, on May 1, 1893. These were illustrations on government printed postal cards and privately printed souvenir cards. The government postal cards had the printed one-cent stamp, while the souvenir cards required a two-cent adhesive postage stamp to be applied. Writing was not permitted on the address side of the cards.

Private Mailing Card Era (1898-1901)

On May 19, 1898, private printers were granted permission, by an act of Congress, to print and sell cards that bore the inscription "Private Mailing Card." Today, we call these cards "PMCs." Postage required was now a one-cent adhesive stamp. A dozen or more American printers began to take postcards seriously. Writing was still not permitted on the address side.

Postcard Era (1901-1907)

The use of the word "Postcard" was granted by the government to private printers on December 24, 1901. Writing was still not permitted on the address side. In this era, private citizens began to take black-and-white photographs and have them printed on paper with postcard backs.

Divided Back Era (1907-1914)

Postcards with a divided back were permitted March 1, 1907. The address was to be written on the right side and the left side was for writing messages. Many millions of cards were published and printed in this era, most in Germany, where printers were far more advanced in the lithographic processes. With the advent of World War I, the supply of postcards had to come from England and the United States.

White Border Era (1915-1930)

Most domestic-use postcards were printed in the United States during this period. To save ink, a border was left around the view, thus the name "White Border Cards." The high cost of labor, inexperience, and public taste created cards of inferior quality. Competition in a narrowing market caused many publishers to go out of business.

Linen Era (1930-1944)

New printing processes allowed printing on postcards with high rag content that caused a linen-like finish. These cheap cards allowed for the use of gaudy dyes for coloring. Curt Teich's line of linen postcards flourished. Many important historical events are recorded on these cards.

Photochrome Era (1945 to present)

The chrome postcards started to dominate the scene soon after they were launched by the Union Oil Company in their western service stations in 1939. Mike Roberts pioneered with his "WESCO" cards soon after World War II. Three-dimensional postcards also appeared during this era.